TH...
MORMONISM

Illumination or Deception?

DENNIS & RAUNI HIGLEY

THE TRUTH ABOUT MORMONISM
published by The Berean Call

Questions and comments may be addressed to:

Dennis and Rauni Higley
P.O. Box 900415
Sandy, Utah 84093-0415
email: hismin@xmission.com
website: www.hismin.com

© 2012 by Dennis and Rauni Higley

First edition 2001 • Second edition 2004 • Third edition 2008
Fourth edition 2012
International Standard Book Number: 978-1-928660-63-7
Library of Congress PCN: 2008934671

Scripture quotations are from:
The Holy Bible, King James Version

COPYRIGHT & FAIR USE

The Berean Call
PO Box 7019
Bend, Oregon 97708-7020
www.thebereancall.org

PRINTED IN THE UNITED STATES OF AMERICA

Contents

INTRODUCTION

A prominent Mormon leader has written a confident statement concerning his faith—a statement every thinking person must take seriously. President Joseph Fielding Smith (the 10th President of the LDS Church) declared:

> Mormonism must stand or fall on the story of Joseph Smith. He was either a Prophet of God, divinely called, properly appointed and commissioned or he was one of the biggest frauds this world has ever seen. There is no middle ground. If Joseph was a deceiver, who willfully attempted to mislead people, then he should be exposed, his claims should be refuted, and his doctrines shown to be false....(*Doctrines of Salvation*, 1:188-89)

When one reads the statement above, an investigation—through a study of the pertinent documentation—is called for. Historically, the Mormon story is a young one, and for that reason alone is relatively easy to investigate.

Try the Spirits

If you believe that the LDS Church is true, you should not fear to investigate it, but welcome the challenge. The truth will not change. Only lies have to be protected and hidden.

If we have made any errors in our presentation of facts we have learned, we would like to know so that we can correct them. We have documented for you some samples of our studies in the history of the LDS Church, its doctrines and claims. Study them and see if they are correct.

Beloved, believe not every spirit, but try the spirits whether they are of God: because many false prophets are gone out into the world.

—1 JOHN 4:1

Chapter 1

HISTORICAL BEGINNINGS

Joseph Smith claimed that he had a visit from God the Father and His Son, Jesus Christ, in 1820. He said they told him that all churches were wrong and were an abomination to God and that he should not join any of them. He said that when he told his community about God's visit, it initiated his fierce persecution.

Later he said that he received visits from the angel Moroni who, Joseph Smith said, was a resurrected being who had died close to Smith's area in New York State about 1,400 years earlier. Moroni, Joseph Smith asserted, had buried a record of his people (who allegedly lived on the American continent from about 600 BC to about 421 A.D.) in New York, in the Hill Cumorah. That record, Joseph Smith was told, would be given to him to translate. A few years later, Joseph Smith said that he received the record written on gold plates in "reformed Egyptian" —a language that no one but he could understand. He was also told not to show these gold plates to anyone but that at a later date, a few selected people would be given the privilege to view them. He said that he then translated the plates and published the material as the Book of Mormon and gave the gold plates back to the angel Moroni.

The Church of Jesus Christ of Latter-day Saints claims that the name of the church was given to Joseph Smith by revelation. When Smith first organized the church in 1830, however, it was called the Church of Christ. Four years later the name was changed to the Church of Latter-day Saints. In 1838 it was changed again, this time to The Church of Jesus Christ of Latter-day Saints, as it is known today.

Joseph Smith claimed that he received many revelations from God, and he began to introduce many new doctrines to his new Church; one of the doctrines was polygamy, a practice that Smith denied publicly but practiced secretly. That doctrine was the obvious downfall of Joseph Smith, and he was killed in 1844 as a result of the polygamy controversy.

Now let's go back and look at the above information a little closer and in detail.

Joseph Smith claimed that after he had seen a vision of God the Father and Jesus Christ, he told it first to a Methodist preacher, and that started the entire community, "all men of high standing" and "the great ones of the most popular sects," to persecute him bitterly—he being only a boy of 14! One would think that kind of commotion would have caused someone somewhere to write about it. One would think that at least the Palmyra newspaper would have written something, since Joseph Smith claimed that "all men" were united to bring "bitter and reviling persecution" against him. Not many important events took place in that little town—even unimportant gossip was printed—but one searches in vain, from 1820 on, to find an account about a young boy's vision or persecution.

A search also fails to find a story regarding the revival excitement that Smith later claimed was the reason he went to the grove to seek God in prayer and where he received this fantastic vision. Joseph Smith said that he was told twice in this vision not to join any of the religions (see *The Pearl of Great Price: Joseph Smith—History* 1:5-26); however, it is interesting to note that in 1823 Joseph's mother, sister, and two brothers joined the Presbyterian Church, and Joseph himself later sought membership in the Methodist Church, where his wife was a member. Records show that Joseph was expelled in 1828 because of his belief in magic and also because of his "money-digging activities."

Joseph's newly organized church started to publish its history, as events took place, in a publication called the *Messenger and Advocate*. Oliver Cowdery was the main writer, and its accuracy was checked by Joseph Smith himself. In this publication, Joseph tells how—after his brother Alvin's death, and after his mother, sister, and two brothers had joined the Presbyterian Church—he started to seek religion and to pray "if some Supreme Being existed" (*Messenger and Advocate* 1:79). (If he had had a vision of God the Father and His Son Jesus Christ in 1820, he most certainly would have known by 1823 or 1824 that a Supreme Being existed.) By reading diaries, records, newspapers, etc., one seeks in vain to find any mention of this so-called "First Vision" story until 1842, when it was published in *Times and Seasons,* 22 years after this vision supposedly took place. It becomes quite obvious that this report was an afterthought, since "the Vision-story" talks about two separate gods, and the Book of Mormon says that there is only one God, and that Jesus, God the Father, and the Holy Ghost are this one God. (Examples: Alma 11:26-33; 18:26-28; Mosiah 15:1,2,5, etc.)

The *Doctrine and Covenants* (hereafter noted as *D&C*), (previously called the *Book of Commandments*) was published in 1835 and it included *The Lectures of Faith,* given in the School of the Prophets, named in the title page of the *D&C* as "Theology, the Doctrine of the Church of The Latter Day Saints, Section I." (These *Lectures of Faith,* containing seven lectures, were approved by a Conference vote of the Mormon Church, August 17, 1835, and were included in all English editions of the *D&C* until 1921, when they were—without explanation or vote—removed.) *Lecture 5* says that God is a

Spirit and only the Son has a body of flesh and bones. The *Lectures* are available as a separate small book, with an added footnote to *Lecture 5*, reporting that Joseph Smith received "further light" on April 2, 1843 (see *D&C* 130:22), and only *then* came to know that God the Father also had a body of flesh and bones. That statement alone reveals that there was no vision of the Father and the Son in 1820. Had there been one, Joseph would not have needed "further light" to learn, 23 years after this famed "First Vision," about the Father also having a body of flesh and bones.

It was not until 1844 that Joseph started to preach about a god who was once a man and progressed into godhood, and how men can also become gods (see *Teachings of the Prophet Joseph Smith*, pp. 345-47). Thus, there is absolutely no evidence for the "First Vision" as it appears in *The Pearl of Great Price* or that The Vision was known to Mormons or non-Mormons prior to 1842, when it was published for the first time. It was not until the 1880s that this story was accepted by the Church. Prior to that time, we are able to read only denials about it. For example, in *Journal of Discourses* 2:171 (hereafter *J of D*), Brigham Young preached a sermon in 1855, in which he said,

> Lord did not come...to Joseph Smith, but sent His angel...to inform him that he should not join any religious sect of the day, for they were all wrong....

John Taylor later said the same thing (see *J of D*: 20:167) on March 2, 1879. Heber C. Kimball said in *J of D* (6:29),

> Do you suppose that God in person called upon Joseph Smith, our prophet? God called upon him, but did not come Himself....

George A. Smith told the same story in *J of D* (12:33-34). One wouldn't really have to dig any deeper than that to find out that the claims of the LDS Church today regarding Joseph Smith's so-called "First Vision" are not true, according to documentary evidence of the time. Joseph Smith—and these facts —should be exposed, just as Joseph Fielding Smith said they should be.

Early Mormon apostle Orson Pratt made a statement concerning the Book of Mormon:

> This book (Book of Mormon) must be either true or false. If true, it is one of the most important messages ever sent from God....If false, it is one of the most cunning, wicked, bold, deep-laid impositions ever palmed upon the world, calculated to deceive and ruin millions.... The nature of the message in the Book of Mormon is such that, if true, no one can possibly be saved and reject it; if false, no one can possibly be saved and receive it...if, after a rigid examination, it be found imposition, it should be extensively published to the world as such; the evidences and arguments on which the imposture was detected should be clearly and logically stated, that

those who have been sincerely yet unfortunately deceived may perceive the nature of deception, and to be reclaimed, and that those who continue to publish the delusion may be exposed and silenced...by strong and powerful arguments—by evidences adduced from scripture and reason.... (*Orson Pratt's Works, Divine Authenticity of the Book of Mormon*, Liverpool, 1851, pp. 1-2)

In this booklet, we hope to show clearly and logically—even though very briefly—that the Book of Mormon is not a divinely inspired record, but rather is a nineteenth-century product. Joseph Smith claimed that after he translated the gold plates, he returned them to an angel—so there is no way to inspect them or check the accuracy of the translation.

Mormons often refer to the witnesses of the Book of Mormon. Most of these men later left the Church, but claims are also made that even though they did, they never denied that they had seen an angel who showed them "the plates of the Book of Mormon." However, in *J of D* (7:164), Brigham Young stated that

> ...witnesses of the Book of Mormon, who handled the plates and conversed with the angels of God, were afterwards left to doubt and to disbelieve that they had ever seen an angel.

Joseph Smith himself called these men wicked, and liars, and by many other demeaning names. In *J of D* (7:114-15),

George A. Smith lists those who have left the Church and mentions specifically "the witnesses of the Book of Mormon." Martin Harris later claimed that he had a better testimony of the "Shakers Book" than he ever had of the Book of Mormon. Reading about these witnesses, one is drawn to the conclusion that they were unstable men and easily convinced. For example, Martin Harris changed his religion at least *eight times*. Some of the others (perhaps taking a cue from Joseph Smith) even started their *own* religious denominations later.

Chapter 2

DIFFICULTIES IN THE BOOK OF MORMON

The Book of Mormon presents difficulties that cannot be explained away regarding the following topics:

Language

First Nephi 1:2, etc., states that Hebrews who left Jerusalem and came to the Americas spoke Egyptian. It is a known fact that Hebrews spoke Hebrew, and their records were kept in Hebrew. Egyptians were their enemies. It is as absurd to think that Hebrews would have written their sacred history in Egyptian as to think that American history would have been written in Russian! In Mormon 9:32, 34, it is stated that the language was "reformed Egyptian" and that no other people knew their language. There is no known language called "reformed Egyptian."

Desert Fruit

First Nephi 17:5 talks about ample fruit and wild honey being products of the Sinai Desert (called Bountiful). Not possible!

Desert Timber

First Nephi 18:1 talks about ample timber that these Jews used to build a ship. There is not ample timber in that area. It was a desert. It is still a desert.

Laman River

First Nephi 2:6-9 mentions a river named Laman that flows into the Red Sea. There is no river there, nor has there been one since the Pleistocene Era (even if one accepts evolutionary geology).

Botanical Problems

Discrepancies abound in the Book of Mormon. Wheat, barley, olives, etc., are mentioned, but none of these were in the Americas at that time.

Animals

North America had no cows, asses, horses, oxen, etc.; Europeans brought them hundreds and hundreds of years later. North America had no lions, leopards, or sheep at that time. Honey bees were brought here by Europeans much later. Ether 9:18,19 lists domestic cattle, cows and oxen as separate species! They did not even exist in the Americas at that time, nor did chickens, dogs, or elephants.

And what on earth are "curloms" and "cumoms"? No such animals have ever been identified anywhere. Domestic animals that are thought to be "useful" would hardly become extinct.

Butter is also mentioned, but it could not possibly have existed, since no milk-producing animals were found in the Americas at that time.

Clothing Material

The Book of Mormon mentions silk and wool clothing, but they did not exist at that time, nor did moths (1 Nephi 13:7; Alma 46, Ether 9:17; 10:24).

Beheaded Shiz

Ether 15:30-31 says that after Shiz (the Jaredite military leader) was beheaded, "Shiz raised upon his hands and fell; and after that he had struggled for breath, he died."

Miscalculation

In Ether, chapter 6, we learn that furious winds propelled the barges to the Promised Land for 344 days! Even if the winds were not "furious" but, for example, blew only 10 miles per hour, the distance traveled in 344 days would have been 82,560 miles, or more than *three times* around the world. Absurdity, to say the least!

Engineering Flaw

Furthermore, why would the Lord instruct the brother of Jared to make a hole on the top and *bottom* of each barge (Ether 2:20)?

Population

When Lehi left Jerusalem, according to the Book of Mormon, his group consisted of perhaps fewer than 20 people. Yet 19 years later the people had so prospered and multiplied in the Promised Land that they built a temple of which the "manner of construction was like unto the temple of Solomon: and the workmanship thereof was exceeding fine" (2 Nephi 5:16)—see chapter 3 for further details.

Looking at what the Bible says about the construction of Solomon's temple, we find that it took 30,000 Israelites, 150,000 hewers of stone and carriers, 3,300 supervisors (1 Kings 5:13-16), and about seven years to build it (see also 1 Kings 6).

How many people could Lehi have had in his group after 19 years? Most of them would have still been very young children or teenagers, hardly capable of building a temple.

The book further explains that in fewer than 30 years after arriving on this continent, they had multiplied so rapidly that they divided into two nations. Even the most rapid human reproduction could have resulted in only a few dozen in that brief time, and most of them still would be infants or small children, and about one-third older people.

Not only did they divide into two nations, but throughout the book, every few years, they had devastating wars that killed thousands (i.e., Alma 28:2).

Skin Color

After the first 19 or so years, Laman and Lemuel and their descendants and followers(!) turned dark skinned because of their disobedience (2 Nephi 5:21). According to the Book of Mormon, a dark skin color was a curse from God. This change of skin color takes place throughout the book. In 2 Nephi 30:6, we read that if Lamanites accepted the gospel, they would become "white and delightsome" (and, since the 1981 printing of the Book of Mormon, we read that they became "pure and delightsome"), and if they "dwindled in unbelief they became a dark and loathsome..." (1 Nephi 12:23). People's skin color does not change if they believe or do not believe, nor is skin color a curse!

The Book of Mormon teaches that Native Americans originated from these Jewish settlers. However, Native Americans are distinctly Mongoloid. They have the "Mongoloid" blue spot, specific blood traits, and their facial features are of typical Asian origin, not Semitic at all.

DNA testing and studies of the Indian tribes (that the LDS Church and the Book of Mormon teach to be "Lamanites"), have concluded that American Indians are Mongoloids from Siberia and not Hebrews from Jerusalem. Nearly 100 years of scientific research has refuted all claims of the Book of Mormon, which is believed by the LDS to be an actual history of millions of Semitic people who built magnificent cities and had an advanced culture. Due to these testing results, the LDS Church saw it necessary (Nov. 2007) to change the wording on the Introduction page to the Book of Mormon—written in 1981, they say, "only as a commentary" by Mormon apostle Bruce R. McConkie.

It originally said, "After thousands of years, all were destroyed except Lamanites, and they are the *principal* ancestors of the American Indians."

It will *now* say, "After thousands of years, all were destroyed except the Lamanites, and they are *among* the ancestors of the American Indians." With this change, they are trying to reduce "the Lamanites" to so small a group that they may never be found, and that "the Lamanites" have somehow been absorbed into Indian tribes that now show only Mongoloid DNA. This is contrary to what all LDS prophets from Joseph Smith to the current LDS prophet, Gordon B. Hinckley, have repeatedly stressed: namely, that all American Indians are Lamanites. LDS prophet Spencer W. Kimball emphasized, "[The] term 'Lamanite' includes *all Indians* and

Indian mixtures...Lehi and his family became ancestors of *all* of the Indian and Mestizo tribes in North and South and Central America and in the islands of the sea" (*Ensign*, July 1971, p. 7, emphasis added).

LDS apologists from BYU are also saying that there were a lot of other people on this continent when Lehi and his group arrived. By saying that, they contradict the Book of Mormon that says that this land (American Continent) was "kept from all other nations" (2 Nephi 1:9).

Regardless, this word change to the Introduction to the Book of Mormon does not make a bit of difference because the Title Page to the Book of Mormon says basically the same thing that the Introduction page said – connecting *all Lamanites* to Hebrews. The Title page says that the Book of Mormon "is the record of the people of Nephi, and also of the Lamanites—Written to the Lamanites, who are remnant of the house of Israel...."

This should not be changed, because Joseph Smith said that the Title Page is part of the gold plates and that "it is a literal translation taken...of...the book of plates...this title page is not by any means a modern composition either of mine or any other man's who has lived or does live in this generation" (*Times and Season*, vol. 3, No. 24, p. 943).

JOSEPH SMITH'S ACCOUNT OF THOSE WHO WENT TO
THE "PROMISED LAND" IN 590 BC

Table accompanies Chapter 3 — Summary on page 30

LEHI & SARIAH

| Laman | Lemuel | Sam | Nephi | Sister #1 | Sister #2 | Jacob | Joseph |

ZORAM

Ishmael dies (1 Nephi 16:34). His daughters married Lehi's sons.
Zoram married the eldest daughter of Ishmael (1 Nephi 16:7).

ISHMAEL & WIFE

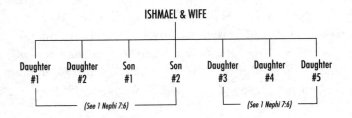

| Daughter #1 | Daughter #2 | Son #1 | Son #2 | Daughter #3 | Daughter #4 | Daughter #5 |

(See 1 Nephi 7:6)   *(See 1 Nephi 7:6)*

Chapter 3

TROUBLE IN
THE FAMILY TREE

The Account of Lehi and Sariah

Mormons tend to assume that Lehi arrived here in the Americas with a great number of people. Let's look at what the Book of Mormon has to say about that and the number of people who could have come here to start this civilization (2 Nephi 1:9 says that this land was kept from knowledge of other nations, so they were the only ones to occupy this land). Use the chart on page 22 for reference.

Lehi and his family left Jerusalem in 600 BC (1 Nephi 2:4 – date is given as BC 600). How old would Lehi's children have been when they left? Remember, they carried all their belongings, provisions, and their tents with them. No mention is made of any pack animals or camels (1 Nephi 2:4).

They traveled for three days away from Jerusalem (1 Nephi 2:6). Nephi and his brothers were sent back to Jerusalem, packing their tents (1 Nephi 3:9). Nephi claims to be "a man large in stature..." (1 Nephi 4:31). How old could this "man" Nephi be? Being the youngest son, he could not have been more than 20 years old at that time. Assuming that there are 18 months between him and the other brothers, that would make Sam about 21 1/2, Lemuel about 23, and Laman 24 1/2.

All of these men married in the same year, including Zoram (1 Nephi 16:7). Zoram took the oldest of Ishmael's daughters, Laman took the second daughter, Lemuel took the third, Sam took the fourth, and Nephi took the fifth.

The year is now somewhere around 596 BC, making Nephi about 22 years old. Their "women did bear children in the wilderness." They "ate raw meat...their...women gave plenty of suck for their children, and they were strong...even like unto the men" (1 Nephi 17:2). The oldest of these children would be only three or four years old by 592 BC. According to 1 Nephi 17:4, they have been in the wilderness for eight years (see date notation at bottom of page in the Book of Mormon).

They arrive at the seashore (1 Nephi 17:5,6). Assuming that there were 18 months between children, they would all be between infancy and four years old. If all these women had children accordingly, there would now be 13 children, all under the age of four. During these years, Lehi had two more sons, who would be less than eight years of age at this time.

So there are, at most, 15 children (including Lehi's two sons born in the wilderness) and 18 adults. Any mention of Nephi's sisters doesn't come till later. Their ages are unknown. We'll assume that they are younger than Nephi and older than Jacob and Joseph, who were born in the wilderness.

Miraculous Mining, Refining, Ship-building

Nephi is commanded to go up to the mountain and meet with God (1 Nephi 17:7). There he is told how to build a ship and make the tools with which to build it (1 Nephi 17:8-11).

In verses 10-11, he is told where to find ore, and in verse 16 he tells how he made tools to build the ship. There are just 18 adults and several very small children to help him mine, smelt, and manufacture the tools—as well as hunting and gathering food.

First Nephi 18:4 states that they completed the building of the ship and "that the workmanship thereof was exceeding fine." The date at the bottom of the page is about 591 BC—so it has taken them one year, more or less, to mine the ore, smelt it, manufacture the tools, harvest the timber, and construct the ship, in addition to finding and gathering food for all these people. By 590 BC (verse 8), they are setting sail for the "promised land," but no mention is made of how or where they obtained material for the sails. The oldest children of Nephi and his brothers are now about five to six years old.

Arrival in the Promised Land

First Nephi 18:23 describes their arrival at the promised land and the pitching of their tents. The date given at the bottom of the page is 589 BC. The oldest of the children are now six to seven years old.

Verse 24 tells how they immediately tilled the earth and planted the seeds they had brought with them. Remember, these seeds have lain dormant now for years and years since they left Jerusalem. Depending on what seeds they brought and planted, it would take four to six months for a crop to mature and be harvested.

Now that they have harvested a good crop, they have time to explore. It is amazing what they find: verse 25 mentions all kinds of wild beasts, wild goats, and all manner of wild animals, along with cows, oxen, asses, horses, and goats, "which were for the use of men." Also, verse 25 states that they found "all manner of ore, both of gold, and of silver, and of copper."

The very next thing Nephi does at the command of the Lord, is to make plates of this new found gold ore to make a record of his people (1 Nephi 19:1-4). The year is now between 588 and 570 BC, and the children might be from 16 years old down to infants. Half of all these children are girls. In the year 580, Nephi would be 38-40 years old.

A "Growing" Population Problem:
Too Few People

In the year 580, the total population of this group (at most) would be 16 older adults. Ishmael had died before they left for the "promised land" (1 Nephi 16:34), and Lehi's death is reported in 2 Nephi 4:12.

These younger men have been married for about 16 years. Zoram married Ishmael's oldest daughter. They reportedly have only one son. Laman had married Ishmael's second daughter.

The maximum number of children at this point, from single births, would be 11 per couple, based on the number of years they have been married, and each having one child every 18 months: Lemuel, Sam, and Nephi would each have eleven children. Nephi had "sisters," but no mention is made of them marrying, or whom they could have married, for 2 Nephi 1:9 says that this land "was kept from all other nations."

The total number of children would now be 45, at the most, during those 16 years (not including those who may have died at birth or from disease or illness), the oldest of these being 15 years old.

Seven of the adults are women. Two are elderly (Lehi's and Ishmael's wives). The other women are nursing mothers with their hands full, taking care of the small children. That leaves only Nephi's unmarried sisters to help with other tasks.

In 2 Nephi 5:5,6, Nephi is told to flee into the wilderness and take all those who would go with him. He takes his older brother, Sam, and his family, and his two younger brothers, Jacob and Joseph, and his sisters "and all those who would go with me." The greatest possible number of people in Nephi's group would then be 35, most of them very young. The remainder would go with Laman and Lemuel.

After traveling in the wilderness for many days, they again set up their tents (v. 7). They sowed their seeds and "reaped in abundance," and "began to raise flocks, and herds, and animals of every kind" (v. 11).

The people have been in the promised land for eight or nine years, and they have "flocks, and herds and animals of every kind." Remarkably, they have somehow managed to domesticate all these animals while "journeying in the wilderness" in this short period (we are using 580 BC as the midpoint date in this examination).

Let's look at the numbers again: the group has split; Laman and Lemuel, their wives, and around 22 children, along with the sons of Ishmael (group of 28 people), cause Nephi to flee into the wilderness.

There, in the wilderness, Nephi makes "many swords", "after the manner of [the sword of Laban]" (2 Nephi 5:14). This was for protection from the evil brothers, Laman and Lemuel, and their group, "lest by any means the people, who were now called Lamanites, should come upon us and destroy us."

Again, the question has to be asked: From where did he get the ore, and how did he refine it and make swords, considering that his small group had only a few adults, a few teenagers, and the were rest small children?

Second Nephi 5:15 continues by stating that they "built buildings" and worked "in all manner of wood, and of iron, and of copper, and of brass, and of steel, and of gold, and of silver, and of precious ores, which were in great abundance".

Second Nephi 5:16 states that Nephi built a temple "after the manner of the temple of Solomon." He continues by saying that it wasn't quite as nice as Solomon's because all those precious things "were *not* to be found upon the land" (emphasis added)—even though he had stated in the verse immediately previous that they were "in great abundance." Nevertheless, "the workmanship was exceeding fine."

Is it logical or reasonable to believe that such a small band (the Nephites) did all this in addition to raising their "flocks and herds," gathering food for their families, mining for precious metals, refining them, and defending themselves against the Lamanites' attacks?

At this point, the time is reported to be between 588 and 570 BC. If we use the date at the end of the chapter, which is 569-559 BC, Nephi is about 59 years old. The children are now grown. But whom are they marrying?

Summary

Lehi, his wife Sariah and their four sons and two daughters leave Jerusalem in 600 BC and go to the wilderness by the Red Sea. Their plan is to sail to a "land of promise" (1 Nephi 2:20). About 597 BC, Lehi sends his sons back to Jerusalem to acquire records engraved on brass plates to "preserve the language of our fathers" (1 Nephi 3:19; 5:10-13). These records contained the five books of Moses and the history of Israel up to that date. In order to get the records, Nephi kills Laban. Laban's servant, Zoram, goes back with Nephi (1 Nephi 4:17-18, 35). Some time later, Lehi again sends his sons back to Jerusalem to convince Ishmael and his family to join them in the wilderness. Ishmael, his wife, five daughters, and two sons (with their families), come back with them (1 Nephi 7:6). Lehi's youngest sons, Jacob and Joseph, were born "in the wilderness" (1 Nephi 18:7) just before they sailed to the "Promised Land" (591 BC).

The family tree and data given to us by Joseph Smith raise crucial questions about this record: How is it possible to derive the great numbers required to substantiate the alleged civilization built by Nephites, and the rest of the history in the Book of Mormon? What evidence exists to refute claims that the "historical" account in the Book of Mormon is nothing more than elaborate fiction? Can an examination of Mormon archaeology exonerate the testimony of Joseph Smith? That is the subject of the next chapter.

Chapter 4

ARCHAEOLOGICAL
DILEMMAS

Archaeologists have yet to unearth any evidence support-
ing the claims of the Book of Mormon. In Ether 7:8-9,
we read of steel and breakable windows (2:23) in Abraham's
time. Try to explain that to an archaeologist! Steel was not
developed until about 3,000 years later.

At the end of the Book of Mormon, Moroni tells about a
great battle that took place on the Hill Cumorah. More than
200,000 people, armed to their teeth, were killed on that hill.
The story tells about their weapons, breastplates, helmets,
swords, etc. Nothing like that has ever been found on that hill
or anywhere else on this continent. Metal helmets, swords,
etc., do not just disappear in a mere 1,400 years.

Before the LDS Church purchased the Hill Cumorah,
it was literally dug full of deep holes and even caves, but

nothing was ever found. (Brigham Young told about the caves inside of Hill Cumorah and how Joseph and Oliver went in and out of them. Supposedly there were wagon loads of gold plates, Laban's sword, and other items—*J of D*, 19:38).

When people simply "dig for worms" in the Holy Land, they make amazing archaeological discoveries that confirm the Bible as an accurate historical record. By contrast, after painstaking expeditions and excavations, archaeologists have yet to discover even a single city, place, coin, sword, or artifact of any kind that is mentioned in the Book of Mormon.

There are still people in the LDS Church who believe that archaeology has proven, at least to a degree, the Book of Mormon. Some LDS teachers are using video and picture-presentations of ruins from Guatemala, Mexico, and South America, implying that they prove the Book of Mormon, even though they are from an entirely different time period than the Book of Mormon and most are ruins built by idol worshipers who offered human sacrifices.

"Mormon scholars" are directing their historic location research efforts and tours in these lands, which implies that Mayans and others were the peoples that the Book of Mormon talks about—even though what is known about Mayans and their religion does not match what the Book of Mormon says. These assumptions that come from BYU go directly against what the leaders of the Church have said and taught about Book of Mormon locations from Joseph

Smith to current leaders. "From all the evidence in the Book of Mormon, augmented by the testimony of the Prophet Joseph Smith, these final battles took place in the territory known as the United States and in the neighborhood of the Great Lakes and hills of Western New York" (Joseph Fielding Smith, *Doctrines of Salvation*, vol. 3, pp. 240-41, emphasis in original).

The professors of BYU say that even the Hill Cumorah (where Joseph Smith found the gold plates) is in *Guatemala*, or maybe in Mexico. The First Presidency's office, however, continues to state that the Hill Cumorah is in Western New York State, *not* in Guatemala or Mexico. (For more about what the prophets and apostles of the Church have taught about Book of Mormon locations, go to *Doctrines of Salvation*, vol. 3, pp. 232-43, written by Joseph Fielding Smith, the tenth president of the LDS Church.)

Another interesting detail found in the Book of Mormon is that it puts Nephi's Tower near the city of Zarahemla (Helaman 7:10). The LDS Church has located the Tower of Nephi in Spring Hill, Daviess County, Missouri, the place identified as valley of "Adam-ondi-Ahman," where Joseph Smith said that Adam and his posterity lived until the time of Noah.

There is another "pile of stones," besides the remnant of the stones of Nephi's Tower, that Joseph Smith had identified as a remnant of an altar Adam had built some 5,000 years before

(*D&C* 107:52-56; 116; *Mormon Doctrine*, p. 21). Based on this, it would be logical that the researchers for Book of Mormon locations would go by what their scriptures say and what their prophet-leaders have revealed, and look for Zarahemla and Manti and perhaps even other places in Missouri and the Great Lakes area instead of Guatemala or Mexico.

LDS Professor Dee Green, in *Dialogue: A Journal of Mormon Thought*, summer of 1969, pp. 74-78, wrote,

> The first myth we need to eliminate is that Book of Mormon archaeology exists. Titles of books full of archaeological half-truths, dilettanti on peripheries of American archaeology calling themselves Book of Mormon archaeologists regardless of their education, and a Department of Archaeology at BYU devoted to the production of Book of Mormon archaeologists do not insure that Book of Mormon archaeology really exists...no Book of Mormon location is known....Biblical archaeology can be studied, because we know where Jerusalem and Jericho were and are, but we do not know where Zarahemla and Bountiful (nor any location for that matter) were or are....

Many Mormon scholars have faced the truth and fully agree with Professor Green but, sadly enough, this "myth of the Book of Mormon archaeology" still surfaces from the general membership who are not updated on these issues.

Thomas S. Ferguson was a firm believer and was sure

that archaeology would prove the Book of Mormon. He was an attorney and believed that he knew how to weigh the evidence once it was found, and a lot of "evidence" *was* found; but unfortunately for the LDS Church, the "evidence" did not have any connection to the Book of Mormon. Ferguson spent hundreds of thousands of dollars and 25 years of his life as head of the "New World Archaeological Foundation," funded by the Church. In spite of all his efforts, by 1970 he had come to the conclusion that all had been in vain—that Joseph Smith was not a prophet, and that Mormonism was not true.

Here was a man who had devoted his entire life, even before starting this foundation, to Mormonism. He had written a book called *One Fold and One Shepherd* in defense of Mormonism, but he later had to admit that the case against Joseph Smith was absolutely devastating and could not be explained away. Finding out that the Book of Abraham in *The Pearl of Great Price* (an LDS scripture) was not a translation of the papyri, as Joseph Smith had claimed, was perhaps the final straw for him, as well as for many others who were more aware of the problems in Mormonism.

External Sources

Another example is B. H. Roberts, noted historian and a General Authority in the Mormon Church, whose secret manuscript, *Book of Mormon Difficulties*, was published in 1985 by the title *Studies of the Book of Mormon*. Roberts had come

to question the Book of Mormon quite some time before
Ferguson did. His typewritten manuscript of more than 400
pages was written between 1922 and 1933. In this manuscript,
he admitted that the Book of Mormon is in conflict with what
is now known from twentieth-century archaeological investigation about the early inhabitants of America. After going
into a lengthy explanation on impossibilities in the Book of
Mormon, he also says that he has come to discover things
he didn't know earlier in his life—for instance, that Joseph
Smith did have access to a number of books that could have
assisted him and given him ideas for the Book of Mormon.
Roberts tells how Joseph's mother wrote in her book, *History
of the Prophet Joseph Smith*, that long before Joseph had received
the gold plates, he gave...

> Most amusing recitals....He would describe the an-
> cient inhabitants of this continent, their dress, mode of
> traveling, and the animals upon which they rode; their
> cities, their buildings, with every particular; their mode
> of warfare, and also their religious worship. This he
> would do with as much ease, seemingly, as if he had
> spent his whole life among them. (B. H. Roberts, *Studies
> of the Book of Mormon*, p. 243)

Roberts goes on to say that Joseph could have gotten his
information from "knowledge" that existed in the community because of books like Ethan Smith's *View of the Hebrews*,

published nearby in 1823, and Josiah Priest's *The Wonders of Nature and Providence*, published only 20 miles away about one year later. The latter had lots to say about the Hebrew origin of American Indians and their advanced culture and civilization. Roberts then asks,

> Whence comes the young prophet's ability to give these descriptions "with as much ease as if he had spent his whole life" with these ancient inhabitants of America? Not from the Book of Mormon, which is as yet, a sealed book to him....These evening recitals could come from no other source than the vivid, constructive imagination of Joseph Smith, a remarkable power which attended him through all his life. It was as strong and varied as Shakespeare's and no more to be accounted for than the English Bard's. (B. H. Roberts, *Studies of the Book of Mormon*, p. 244)

Prior to publication of *Studies of the Book of Mormon*, B. H. Roberts was known as a great defender of Mormonism, and he is still considered to be one of the greatest scholars the LDS Church has ever had. He wrote the six-volume *Comprehensive History of the Church* and many other works as well. There is much, much more to say as to why the Book of Mormon is not an ancient record but an obvious production of a very intelligent and creative person, Joseph Smith, who "borrowed" from a number of books (including the Bible) to create it.

Chapter 5

DOCTRINAL CONTRADICTIONS

None of the important Mormon doctrines of today are in the Book of Mormon. Yet the Church claims that this book "contains the fullness of the everlasting Gospel." [According to the *D&C* and the General Authorities of the Church, "fullness of the Gospel consists in those laws, doctrines, ordinances, powers, and authorities needed to enable men to gain the fullness of salvation," meaning that all doctrines leading to full salvation in the celestial kingdom are in that book, and one wouldn't need any other books or information on how to gain salvation. (See *D&C* 20:9; 27:5; 42:12; 135: 3; *Mormon Doctrine*, p. 333; 512.)]

As the following examples prove beyond any shadow of doubt, the Book of Mormon, as recorded by Joseph Smith, clearly contradicts today's Mormon doctrine.

Polygamy

"For there shall not any man among you have save it be one wife; and concubines he shall have none;" —Jacob 2:27, also Jacob 1:15; 2:22-27; 3:5; Mosiah 11:2; Ether 10:5. (Note: Polygamy is not practiced by the mainstream LDS Church today, but it remains as doctrine of the Church; see *D&C* 132.)

Eternal Progression

Eternal progression is a doctrine that God has progressed from a man to a god and that men can likewise become gods: "God is the same yesterday, today, and forever, and in him there is no variableness…" —Mormon 9:9, also Alma 41:8, 21; 3 Nephi 24:6; Mormon 9:10,19; Moroni 8:18,23.

"Secret Combinations"

Secret combinations (or oaths Mormons are put under in their temples): "Cursed be the land forever and ever unto those workers of darkness and secret combinations…" — Alma 37:31, also Mormon 8:27; 2 Nephi 9:9; 26:22; Alma 34:36; 37:23.

Creation or Organization?

God created the heaven and the earth by His Word: "By his word the heaven and the earth should be; and by the power of his word man was created of the dust of the earth…" — Mormon 9:17, also Jacob 4:9. [The Mormon Church teaches that God did not create anything by His word but "organized" the world using existing materials. Joseph Smith said that spirit cannot be created or made; i.e., that God did not create the spirit of man at all (*D&C* 93:29; *Teachings*, pp. 350-53; *Mormon Doctrine*, pp. 169-70, 751.)]

One God or Many Gods?

There is only one God: "...Christ the Son, and God the Father, and the Holy Spirit, which is one Eternal God..." — Alma 11:44, also Mosiah 7:27; 13:34; 15:1-5; 16:15; Alma 11:26-33,38,39. Joseph Smith later taught that God was once a man and that God had a God before him, and that men will become gods, thus "plurality of Gods exists." (*Teachings*, pp. 345-347; *Mormon Doctrine*, pp. 319-22; 576-77)

Work for the Dead

There is no work for the dead: Alma 34:32-33. But the LDS Church is almost feverishly building more and more temples to perform "work for the dead," "giving the dead a second chance for salvation," and ignoring not only the Book of Mormon, but also what the Bible says in Hebrews 9:27—declaring that after death comes *judgment* (see also Luke 16:19-31).

Doctrines such as "temple," "eternal marriage," "priesthoods," etc., are not in the Book of Mormon—and, as we have already mentioned, one can see that the Book of

Mormon speaks against polygamy, work for the dead, oaths (temple), men becoming gods, or that there is more than one God, etc. It becomes quite obvious to an investigator of Mormonism that after 1842, Joseph Smith changed his mind about who God is.

Other Examples

Smith contradicted the Book of Mormon, Alma 34:36, that says, "And this I know, because the Lord hath said he dwelleth not in unholy temples, but in the hearts of the righteous doth he dwell...," with *D&C* 130:3: "[T]he idea that the Father and the Son dwell in a man's heart is an old sectarian notion, and is false...."

The Book of Mormon says in Jacob 4:9, "For behold, by the power of his word man came upon the face of the earth, which earth was created by the power of his word. Wherefore, if God being able to speak and the world was, and to speak and man was created...." Joseph Smith changed that and said, "Men who are preaching salvation, say that God created the heavens and earth out of nothing? The reason is, that they are unlearned in the things of God....God never had the power to create the spirit of man at all" (*Teachings*, pp. 350-54). He had begun to teach that his god had once been a mere mortal man, just as he is now.

Chapter 6

THE BOOK OF ABRAHAM

In November 1967, when discovered Egyptian papyri were given back by the New York Metropolitan Museum to the Mormon Church, it generated a great amount of excitement in the hearts of Mormons. Finally, there was something concrete and testable that an "angel didn't take away," which could once and for all prove to the doubting world that Joseph Smith really was a prophet of God and had a God-given gift, or ability, to translate. We read from *The Pearl of Great Price* the following introduction to the Book of Abraham:

> Translated from the papyrus by Joseph Smith, a translation of some ancient records, that have fallen into our hands from the catacombs of Egypt—the writings of Abraham while he was in Egypt, called the Book of Abraham, written by his own hand, upon papyrus.

These papyri were written in the Egyptian language, and this would prove that if Joseph Smith's translation of the papyri was correct, it would be possible that he could have translated the Book of Mormon from "reformed Egyptian." But problems began to surface shortly after the First Presidency had given the papyri to LDS Professor Hugh Nibley of BYU to translate, or to find a translator capable of doing so. (It is of interest to note that it wasn't given to the current prophet, seer, and revelator of the Church.)

Now, if these papyri were written by Abraham "by his own hand," as Joseph Smith had said, they would be at least 4,000 years old. After these papyri were evaluated, even Professor Nibley had to agree that they were a production not any older than the first century A.D. Thus, Abraham could not have written them. That was the first blow. The second blow came after they were given to several qualified Egyptologists to translate; they were clearly shown not to be what Joseph Smith had said the Book of Abraham was. Expectations of Church members had been high, as stated by Dr. Sidney B. Sperry, one of the most noted LDS scholars:

> The little volume of Scripture known as the Book of Abraham will someday be recognized as one of the most remarkable documents in existence. It is evident that writings of Abraham while he was in Egypt, of which our printed Book of Abraham is a copy, must of necessity be older than original text of Genesis....

(Dr. Sidney B. Sperry, *Ancient Records Testify in Papyrus and Stone*, 1938, p. 83, quoted from *Mormonism: Shadow or Reality*, p. 294)

Now that the papyri had been located and proven by the leaders of the Church and its scholars to be the very ones Joseph Smith had translated, the question was, do they read the same as Joseph Smith's translation said? Very quickly they were discovered to be nothing more than pagan burial records called the "Book of Breathings," a short portion of the *Book of the Dead*. Egyptologist James Henry Breasted explains that "...the *Book of the Dead* is chiefly a book of magical charms... it was written by a very superstitious people and is quite different from the religion taught in the Bible" (*Development of Religion and Thought in Ancient Egypt*, New York, 1969, p. 308, as quoted from *Changing World of Mormonism*, Jerald and Sandra Tanner, p. 345). Many Mormon writers have admitted that this is the case:

> There have been a lot of things written and suggestions made trying to justify the fact that not one mention of Abraham, not his name, not his faith, nothing at all are on the document, claimed to have been "written by his [Abraham's] own hand, upon papyrus." (*Pearl of Great Price*, The Book of Abraham)

LDS doctrine on blacks and the priesthood is (was) based on this Book of Abraham. The Utah Mormon Church has not removed this book from their scriptures nor refuted its doctrine on blacks, but it is interesting to note that in the *New York Times*, May 3, 1970, the RLDS Church (currently called the Community of Christ), which at that time was led by the direct descendants of Joseph Smith, made this statement: "It may be helpful to suggest that the Book of Abraham represents simply the product of Joseph Smith's imagination...." The RLDS Church removed the book from among their scriptures. The only change that the Utah Mormon Church made was to allow blacks (in 1978) to have the priesthood.

All in all, thinking people began to see a huge shadow cast on the Book of Mormon. Mormon writer Klaus Hansen made some remarks in *Dialogue: A Journal of Mormon Thought*, Summer 1970, p. 110:

> To a professional historian, for example, the recent translation of the Joseph Smith papyri may well present the potentially most damaging case against Mormonism since its foundation. Yet the "Powers That Be" at the Church Historian's Office should take comfort in the fact that almost total lack of response to this translation is an uncanny proof of Frank Kermode's observation that *even the most devastating acts of disconfirmation will have no effect whatever on true believers.* Perhaps an even more telling response is that of the "liberals," or cultural Mormons. After the Joseph Smith papyri affair, one might have well expected a mass exodus of these people from the Church. Yet none has occurred. Why? *Because cultural Mormons, of course, do not believe in the historical authenticity of Mormon scriptures in the first place. So there is nothing to disconfirm.* (Emphasis added)

Chapter 7

POLYGAMY
AND ADULTERY

olygamy, as we have mentioned at the beginning, was the issue that led to the killing of Joseph Smith. Investigation of the records shows that Joseph Smith had practiced polygamy from the early 1830s on. William Clayton was Joseph Smith's personal secretary and scribe until Joseph's death. Clayton's diary has been a source for many revelations published in *Doctrine and Covenants*.

Revelations in Clayton's Diary

Clayton's diary also tells how the "revelation" on polygamy originated. Stated briefly, this teaching came about as a result of a discussion between Joseph, his brother Hyrum, and William Clayton, who wrote it down. Emma, Joseph's wife, had been suspecting Joseph of having affairs with other women, i.e., Fanny Alger in 1831 or so, and from then on.

As Joseph was relating this to his brother Hyrum and to William in July of 1843, family life was neither very happy nor calm. Hyrum suggested that Joseph write a "revelation" in which God gives instructions for Joseph to have other wives. Joseph doubted that Emma would believe that. William Clayton, however, wrote it down and Hyrum took it to Emma. Emma, of course, did not believe it. Joseph somehow convinced her to accept it for a short time; but after Joseph's death, Emma went into total denial of the polygamy as if it had never happened. (This is also reported on page 151 in *Mormon Enigma: Emma Hale Smith, Prophet's Wife: "Elect Lady," Polygamy's Foe*, written by two LDS women, Linda King Newell and Valeen Tippetts Avery.) Many thought that Emma's reasons were to protect her children and the memory of their father.

Utah LDS Church historian Andrew Jensen, in 1887, taking from the enormous files of then-secret manuscript material in the Salt Lake City Church Library, compiled the first list of 27 wives of Joseph Smith. Genealogical Archives were used to add another 21. Nauvoo Temple records were the main source.

Why Were the Church Records Altered?

Fanny Alger was Joseph Smith's first plural wife, married to Joseph in early 1833. *D&C* of 1890 says that the revelation was *given* July 12, 1843. *History of the Church*, 5:500-501, also says that it was *given* that day, but the current *D&C*, Section

132, says that it was *recorded* July 12, 1843—implying that it could have been given at an earlier date.

This kind of altering of the records of the Church can be noticed quite often by comparing earlier printings with more recent ones. Obvious attempts were made to save some integrity, since it was known that Joseph Smith had been a polygamist a full decade before 1843.

This alteration of the records did not bolster his image, since he and the Church leaders had denied polygamy publicly but practiced it secretly. In the first edition of *Doctrine and Covenants*, printed in 1835, in Section 101:4 there is a denial of polygamy, calling it a "crime of fornication...." This denial of polygamy remained in the *D&C* until 1876, when it was removed and Section 132 was added—the section about God *commanding* the practice of polygamy! Section 132 is still in the *D&C*.

Can Women Have Multiple Living Husbands?

Joseph Smith (and later, Brigham Young as well), were even married to women who were other men's wives. Historical records of these strange marriages are available. According to these records, nine of the first twelve polygamous wives of Joseph Smith were at the same time also married to other men, and he took at least two more married women as his wives. A few examples might be appropriate to present here:

- **Prescinda Huntington Buell,** wife of Norman Buell, later also a wife of Heber C. Kimball, married Norman Buell in 1827, and they had two children. Joseph married her in the fall of 1838 and had a child by her. She continued to be married to Buell as well.

- **Nancy Marinda Johnson Hyde,** wife of Orson Hyde, was also one of Joseph's wives. That caused Orson Hyde to leave the Church for awhile, but he later came back. Genealogical Archives in Salt Lake City show that Nancy Hyde was sealed to Joseph Smith on July 30, 1857, years after Joseph Smith's death.

- **Zina Diantha Huntington Jacobs,** later wife of Brigham Young, was married to Henry Jacobs on March 7, 1841, and seven and one-half months later to Joseph Smith on October 27, 1841. Zina never divorced her husband Henry Jacobs, but after Joseph's death, Brigham publicly told Jacobs, "The woman you claim for a wife does not belong to you. She is a spiritual wife of brother Joseph, sealed to him. I am his proxy, and she, in his behalf, with her children, *are my property*. You can go where you please and get another..." (*Rocky Mountain Saints* by T.B.H. Stenhouse," pp. 185-86; emphasis added). Jacobs obviously accepted Brigham's decision, for he stood as a witness when, in the Nauvoo Temple in January 1846, Zina was sealed to Brigham Young for "time," and Joseph Smith for "eternity."

- **Mary Elizabeth Rollins Lightner,** wife of Adam Lightner, later claimed that Joseph had told her that an angel came to him in 1834 with a drawn sword and commanded him to take her as his wife. She was then only 17. In her diary, she wrote that she was sealed and married to Joseph in the Masonic Hall in Nauvoo in 1842. She was later also married to Brigham Young while remaining married to Adam Lightner. They later moved to Utah. She remained in the Church, even though her husband never joined the Church.

Andrew Jensen did this research in 1887 to prove that Joseph Smith did practice polygamy, since the RLDS Church was denying that he ever did. (For more information on Joseph Smith and his plural wives, read *In Sacred Loneliness: Plural Wives of Joseph Smith*, by LDS professor Todd Compton, Signature Books 1998.) In 1838, when Oliver Cowdery had accused Joseph of these adulterous affairs, Joseph had Oliver excommunicated.

What Was the True Cause of Joseph's Murder?

The controversy over polygamy was the underlying reason for the death of Joseph Smith and his brother Hyrum. William Law's wife had confessed that she had had an affair with Joseph. William Law left the Church and started a publication called *Nauvoo Expositor*. One issue was published and the second one was going to print when Joseph learned that Law was going to have his wife's confession in that issue. Joseph had the press destroyed and the building burned. That caused his arrest and, consequently, his death, but he did not die as "a martyr," as is claimed. John Taylor, third president of the Church, who was in the prison with Joseph and Hyrum at the time, tells the following in *Gospel Kingdom*, p. 360:

> Joseph opened the door slightly, and snapped the pistol six successive times...afterwards [I] understood that two or three were wounded by these discharges, two of whom, I am informed, died.

The same account is also found in *History of the Church*, volume 6: 617-18 and on Introduction to volume 6: XLI.

It was too bad that Joseph Smith was thus killed, but he did not die as a martyr who went "as a lamb to the slaughter," as is claimed by the LDS Church. He died in a gunfight and killed two people before he was shot.

Joseph responded as a Mason, seeking help from Masons, at the time of his death. John Taylor tells that Joseph went to the window and made the Masonic distress sign after his gun was empty, hoping that Masons, if there were any among this mob, would rescue him according to the Masonic oath, "to defend one another, right or wrong."

Chapter 8

THE TEMPLE CEREMONY

The Mormon temple ceremony compares quite precisely with the Masonic ceremony—signs, tokens, and penalties included. However, some changes to the LDS temple ceremony were instituted in April of 1990 to make it less frightening to initiates.

Joseph, Hyrum, Brigham, and others were Masons. Six weeks after Joseph Smith had received his "sublime (Masonic) degree" (see *History of the Church*, vol. 4:552) he introduced his followers to a very similar ceremony, announcing that he had "received [it] as a revelation from God." Dr. Reed Durham, Director of the LDS Institute of Religion, made public his discovery when he spoke on the subject of the Mormon-Mason connection to the Utah History Association on April 20, 1974. He was later highly criticized for making this matter public.

Dr. Durham also showed Joseph's Jupiter talisman and explained that Joseph had carried it on his person from 1826 on (the same year he was convicted of money-digging charges and being a believer in magic) and that the Jupiter talisman was found on him at the time of his death. Other magical items, which belonged to Hyrum Smith, were exposed at the same time. The Patriarch of the Church, Eldred G. Smith, direct descendant of Hyrum Smith, supposedly has them in his possession.

By the way, what has happened to the office of the Patriarch to the Church, a position last held by Patriarch Eldred G. Smith?

> Of the patriarchs to the church the Lord says "He shall hold the keys of the patriarchal blessings upon the heads of all my people." As one of the General Authorities, the patriarch to the Church stands next in order to the members of the Council of the Twelve. (*Mormon Doctrine*, 1966 ed., pp. 560-61; *D&C* 124:91-94)

Who now holds the keys of the patriarchal blessings "upon the heads of all my people?"

No one.

Chapter 9

BRIGHAM YOUNG
and
THE ADAM-GOD DOCTRINE

Teachings of the LDS Church became even stranger after Brigham Young led the Mormons to the Salt Lake Valley. There, they thought, they were free to practice what had been illegal elsewhere; i.e., polygamy and blood atonement.

Brigham Young made polygamy public from 1852 on in Utah, even though the LDS Church still denied it outside of Utah. From this same year forward, Brigham started to teach that "Adam is God and Father and the only God with whom we have to do" and that Adam was the father of human spirits as well as Jesus' physical father (for these, see *Journal of Discourses*, 1:50-51; 4:1; 5:331-32, etc).

The LDS Church has issued denials saying that the Adam-God doctrine was never taught, but records clearly show that Brigham Young taught it, not by just mentioning it once or twice, but from 1852 until his death in 1877. Let's look at some of his statements:

> Now hear it, O inhabitants of the earth, Jew and Gentile, Saint and sinner! When our father Adam came into the garden of Eden, he came into it with a celestial body, and brought Eve, one of his wives, with him. He helped to make and organize the world. He is Michael, the Archangel, the Ancient of Days! About whom holy men have written and spoken—He is our Father and our God, and the only God with whom we have to do. Every man upon the earth, professing Christian or non-professing, must hear it, and will know it sooner or later...the earth was organized by three distinct characters, namely Eloheim, Yahovah, and Michael, these three forming a quorum, as in heavenly bodies, and in organizing element, perfectly represented in the Deity, as Father, Son and Holy Ghost. (*J of D*, 1:50-51)

This teaching was repeated and carried on in other Church writings throughout the years. For example, in the *Millennial Star*, vol. 17:195, we read,

> Every knee shall bow, and every tongue confess that he (Adam) is God of the whole earth. Then will the words of the prophet Brigham Young, when speaking

of Adam, be fully realized—"He is our Father and our God, and the only God with whom WE have to do."

Elder James A. Little counselled: "I believe in the principle of obedience; and if I am told that Adam is our Father and our God, I just believe it" (*Millennial Star*, vol. 16:530, as reported in *Mormonism, Shadow or Reality*, p. 174). The records show that there were only two leaders in the Church who had difficulty with this doctrine, namely, apostles Orson Pratt and Amasa Lyman. In one of Brigham's sermons, printed in the *Deseret News*, June 14, 1873, Brigham declared,

> How much unbelief exists in the minds of the Latter-day Saints in regard to one particular doctrine which I revealed to them, and WHICH God revealed to me—namely that Adam is our Father and God.... Our Father Adam helped to make this earth, it was created expressly for him. He brought one of his wives with him. Who is he? He is Michael....He was the first man on earth, and its framer and maker. He with the help of his brethren brought it into existence....Then he (Adam) said: "I want my children that were born to me in the spirit world to come here and take tabernacles of flesh that their spirits may have a house, a tabernacle or a dwelling place as mine has.

For more than 20 years, Brigham Young clearly taught as a doctrine the following:

- Adam was not made of the dust of this earth
  (*Journal of Discourses*, 2:6)

- Adam is the only God with whom we have to do
  (*Journal of Discourses*, 1:50)

- Adam is the Father of our spirits (*Deseret News*, 14
  June 1873)

- Adam was the Father of Jesus Christ (*Journal of
  Discourses*, 1:50-51)

Heber C. Kimball, the First Counselor to Brigham
Young, also taught,

> I have learned by experience that there is but one
> God that pertains to this people, and he is the God that
> pertains to this earth—the first man. That first man
> sent his own son to redeem the world.... (*Journal of
> Discourses*, 4:1)

Brigham Young had claimed that God himself had revealed this doctrine to him. Brigham also had claimed that
his sermons were "as good as scripture" (*J of D* 13:166). If
that is so, then how can the LDS Church today logically reject
his teachings that he said he received from his God? Who was
Brigham's God?

Joseph Smith had said, "Some revelations are from God;
some revelations are of man; and some are of the devil..."
("Address to All Believers in Christ," p. 31). Who determines

the source of the revelations—the followers or the prophet himself?

Further, if Brigham Young was wrong in this fundamental doctrine of who God is, how can the current LDS Church accept him as an authority of God? The LDS Church teaches that there must be an unbroken link of true prophets after the restoration, otherwise the authority would be lost. Contradicting Brigham Young now only proves the incredibility of both the current LDS Church and Brigham Young, and breaks the link to the claimed restoration by Joseph Smith.

One could go on and on about these teachings that clearly show the non-Christian nature of the LDS Church, but let's look at what the LDS Church today teaches about Adam. In *Doctrine and Covenants* 27:11 and 116, Adam is referred to as the "Ancient of Days," spoken of by Daniel the prophet (Daniel 7:9-14). But the Ancient of Days is one of the names of GOD ALMIGHTY of the Bible, not Adam. There is absolutely no question about that! There is also no question that the LDS Church believes and teaches that Adam is the Ancient of Days, who will judge the world. Apostle Bruce R. McConkie, in his book, *Mormon Doctrine,* page 34, says:

> Adam is known as the Ancient of Days....In this capacity he will yet sit in formal judgment upon "ten thousand times ten thousand...."

In the temple ceremony, the Archangel Michael is one of the creators of the world and he then "becomes" Adam.

According to Mormonism, "GODS" "organized" the world (see *The Pearl of Great Price*, Abraham 4 and 5), Adam being one of the three gods presented in the temple ceremony. In plain language, Mormon doctrine clearly implies that Adam is God—a belief documented in other LDS writings.

Chapter 10

THE GOD *and* CHRIST
of MORMONISM

What does the LDS Church teach about Jesus Christ? First of all, we have already documented that Brigham Young taught that Jesus was a spirit child of Adam and spirit brother of all humankind, as well as a brother of angels, even fallen ones—i.e., Jesus is a brother of Lucifer. Brigham further taught that Jesus was also physically a son of Adam, who, as an exalted resurrected being, had come to Mary and fathered Jesus. Brigham emphasized that Jesus was not begotten by the Holy Ghost, as the Bible says.

The LDS Church does not say anymore that Jesus is the son of Adam, both in body and spirit, but they do teach that Jesus is an elder brother of all mankind and a physical son of God the Father, who conceived Jesus "naturally"; thus Jesus was not begotten by the Holy Ghost! This teaching shows that the Jesus of the LDS Church is not "Emmanuel," "God with us," God who, according to the Bible (Matthew 1:23; John 1:1, 14), became a man in order to be our Redeemer. Jesus of the LDS Church is a created being who also had to be redeemed "to work out his own salvation." Jesus of the Bible is the Creator—uncreated, eternal God, who created everything, including Lucifer (John 1:3; Colossians 1:16).

The current teachings of the LDS Church have not changed in this matter. President Ezra Taft Benson, in his book *Come Unto Christ*, page 4, noted:

> The body in which He performed his mission in the flesh was *sired* by that Holy Being we worship as God, our Eternal Father. Jesus was not the son of Joseph, nor was He begotten by the Holy Ghost. He is the Son of the Eternal Father. (Emphasis added)

Apostle Bruce R. McConkie, on page 742 of *Mormon Doctrine*, says,

> God the Father is a perfected, glorified, holy Man, an immortal Personage. And Christ was born into the world as the literal Son of this Holy Being; he was born in the same personal, real, and literal sense that any mortal son is born to a mortal father. There is nothing figurative about this paternity; he was *begotten*, *conceived* and born in the normal and natural course of events, for he is the Son of God, and that designation means what it says.

In the same book, pages 546-47, McConkie says further, under the heading, "Only Begotten Son":

> Each word is to be understood literally. Only means only; Begotten means begotten; and Son means son. Christ was begotten by an Immortal Father *in the same way that mortal men are begotten by their mortal fathers.* (Emphasis added)

This is not what the Bible says. The Bible says that *a Virgin will conceive* and bring forth a Son, who is called Emmanuel, meaning "God with us" (Matthew 1:18-23) — *not an elder brother with us!*

The Mary of the LDS Church was not a virgin who brought forth a son, but a "wife" of the Heavenly Father whom Brigham declared and named to be Adam. LDS Apostle, Orson Pratt, explains in his doctrinal book *The Seer*, page 158,

> The fleshly body of Jesus required a Mother as well as a Father. Therefore, the Father and Mother of Jesus, *according to the flesh* must have been associated together in the capacity of *Husband and Wife; hence the Virgin Mary must have been for the time being, the lawful wife of God the Father*. Inasmuch as *God was the first husband to her* (Mary), it may be that He only gave her to be the wife of Joseph while in this mortal state, and that He intended after the resurrection to again take her as one of his own wives to raise up immortal spirits in eternity....(Emphasis added)

The leaders of the LDS Church have also taught that *their Jesus was married* and had children, and that He was even a polygamist. Again, Apostle Orson Pratt, in *The Seer*, page 172, declares:

> The great Messiah who was the founder of the Christian religion was a Polygamist...the Messiah chose to take upon himself his seed; and by marrying many honorable wives himself, show to all future generations that he approved the plurality of Wives under Christian dispensation....The son followed the example of his Father, and became the great Bridegroom to whom kings' daughters and many of the honorable Wives were to be married. We have also proved that both God the Father and our Lord Jesus Christ inherit their wives in eternity as well as in time.

In answer to the question, "Was Jesus married?" Joseph Fielding Smith, president of the LDS Church in the 1970s, said, "Yes! but do not throw pearls to the swine!" The LDS Church believes that Jesus was married but doesn't want to "throw pearls to the swine"—in other words, to reveal this to non-Mormons.

LDS President Gordon B. Hinckley made a statement June 4, 1998, acknowledging that he (and the LDS Church) does not believe in the same Jesus Christ as traditional Christianity. He said, "The traditional Christ of whom they[Christianity] speak is not the Christ of whom I speak.

For the Christ of whom I speak had been revealed in this the Dispensation of the Fullness of Times. He, together with His Father, appeared to the boy Joseph Smith in the year 1820, and when Joseph left the grove that day, he knew more of the nature of God *than all the learned ministers* of the gospel of the ages" (*Church News*, June 20, 1998, p. 7; emphasis added).

In the LDS Church's 147th General Conference, General Authority Bernard P. Brockbank stated that the Christ followed by the Mormons is *not* the Christ followed by traditional Christianity. He explains:

> It is true that many of the Christian churches worship *a different Jesus Christ* than is worshipped by the Mormons.... (*The Ensign*, May 1977, p. 26; emphasis added)

In summary, the Jesus of the LDS Church is not the Jesus of the Bible. The God of the LDS Church is not the God of the Bible. Joseph Smith said that there is "a God *above the Father* of our Lord Jesus Christ...." In *Mormon Doctrine*, p. 322, we read,

> If Jesus Christ was the Son of God, and...God the Father of Jesus Christ had a Father, you may suppose that he had a Father also. Where was there ever a son without a father?...Hence if Jesus had a Father, can we not believe that he [the Father] had a Father also?

In 1844, Joseph Smith, as recorded in *Teachings of the Prophet Joseph Smith*, pp. 344-47, told his audience that "*Every man has a natural, and, in our country, a constitutional right to be a false prophet, as well as a true one....*" He continues on the next page, "I am going to tell you how God came to be God. We have imagined and supposed that God was God from all eternity. I will refute that idea and take away the Veil, so that you may see." He then explains, "God himself was once as we are now...and you got to learn how to be Gods yourselves...the same as all Gods have done before you..." (Emphasis added).

Mormon Gods and the "Martyrdom" of Joseph Smith

The God of the Bible says, "Is there a God beside me? Yea, there is no God; *I know not any*" (Isaiah 44:8). If God had a father, and *he* had a father, and so on, the God of the Bible surely would know that!

In the Bible, God calls us to *know*, to *believe*, and to *understand* who He is. God says,

> Ye are my witnesses, saith the LORD, and my servant whom I have chosen: that ye may *know* and *believe* me, and understand that I am he: before me there was no God formed, neither shall there be after me." (Isaiah 43:10)

To Joseph Smith and to all Mormons: the message is clear. There is no other God (or gods)—and therefore, *Mormons will never become a god!* Furthermore, no human being can ever "learn" how to become god, nor attain it by mystic ritual! The God of the Bible says so:

> I am the LORD, and there is none else, there is no God beside Me. (Isaiah 45:5)

God tells what happens to the false prophets who try to lead people after other gods:

> If there arise among you a prophet, or a dreamer of dreams, and giveth thee a sign or a wonder, and the sign or the wonder come to pass, wherefore he spoke unto thee, saying, Let us go after other gods which thou hast not known, and let us serve them; thou shalt not hearken unto the word of that prophet, or the dreamer of dreams: for the LORD your God proveth you, to know whether ye love the LORD your God with all your heart and with all your soul. Ye shall walk after the LORD your God, and fear him, and keep his commandments, and obey his voice, and ye shall serve him, and cleave unto him. and that prophet, or that dreamer of dreams, shall be put to death; because he had spoken to turn you away from the LORD your God.... (Deuteronomy 13:1-5)

It is interesting to note that within weeks after Joseph Smith had, in April 1844, preached this sermon (that men will and can become gods, and that God was not God from all eternity), Joseph was killed—or "put to death."

Coincidence?

Or prophetic fulfillment?

As the Orthodox Jews often say, "Coincidence is not a kosher word."

Chapter 11

THE ONE TRUE GOD

The Bible says that God is God "from everlasting to everlasting" (Psalm 90:2), and when speaking about Messiah, God becoming a man (not a man becoming God!), it says,

> For unto us a child is born, unto us a son is given:... and his name shall be called Wonderful, Counsellor, the Mighty God, the everlasting Father, the Prince of Peace (Isaiah 9:6); Art thou not from everlasting, O Lord my God, mine holy one? (Habakkuk 1:12)

Believers in the God of the Bible are given these comforting words: "The eternal God is thy refuge, and underneath are the everlasting arms..." (Deuteronomy 33:27).

To the followers of Joseph Smith, Brigham Young, and today's LDS prophets, we would like to say, as Joshua said to Israel, "...choose you this day whom ye will serve...but as for me and my house, we will serve the LORD" (Joshua 24:15).

In the English Bible (KJV), whenever the word "LORD" is in all-capital letters, it is the name of God in Hebrew represented by the consonants YHWH (Hebrews didn't dare to pronounce it) and is translated both "LORD" and/or "God." When God spoke to Moses, He declared Himself to be the LORD, the Great I AM, and He said that by His name YHWH (JE-HO-VAH) He was not known to Abraham, Isaac, and Jacob. This was the first time that He revealed His name (Exodus 6:3).

Throughout the Bible, the words, "I am the LORD your God" (Exodus 6:7) or "I the LORD God" are used by God to tell the prophet who is the one who is speaking. The word "LORD" (YHWH) and the word "God" (ELOHIYM) are used as in the example above: "I, the LORD God" (not "we," as the Mormon Church teaches). Speaking of the Godhead, *Mormon Doctrine*, page 576, states:

> As each of these persons is a God, it is evident, from this standpoint alone, that *a plurality of Gods exists*. (Emphasis added)

In Hebrew, the word "El" means God. The word "Elohiym" is the plural form of "El" (similarly, the word cherub is singular, and the word cherubim is plural). When we read in our English Bible, "I am the LORD your God," if we put it back into Hebrew it would read, "I am YHWH your Elohiym." One doesn't get two gods from it—only one God.

"Trinity" is not mentioned in the Bible as a word, but a plurality of persons in ONE GOD is clearly demonstrated throughout the Bible. The Bible came to us through Israel. To the Jew there is but one God, YHWH.

Deuteronomy 6:4 is what Jews repeat daily, and with their dying breath say: "Hear, O Israel, the LORD our God is one LORD," or in Hebrew: "Hear, O Israel, YHWH our Elohiym [plural] is one YHWH."

Most people agree that the Father is God. The Bible teaches that Jesus is God (John 1:1,14; 20:28) and that the Holy Ghost is God (see Acts 5:3-4; 1 Corinthians 3:17; 6:19), but the Bible also teaches that there is only one God. In Isaiah 45:5,6,14,18,21,22, God says that there is no other God or LORD. Other examples: Deuteronomy 4:35,39; 32:39; 1 Samuel 2:2; 2 Samuel 7:22; 22:32; 1 Kings 8:60; Psalm 18:31; Jeremiah 10:10; Galatians 3:20; Ephesians 4:6; Mark 12:32,34.

James 2:19 tells us that even the demons know and believe that there is only one God. Why is it that the LDS Church doesn't know or believe that? The LDS Church says that there is more than one God because in Genesis 1:26, God says, "And God said, let us make man in our image...." Note that there is only one image, and the next verse clarifies it by saying, "So God created man in his own image...in the image of God created he them." God of the Bible is Triune God, one God, three Persons, as 1 John 5:7 says, "For there are three that bear record in heaven, the Father, the Word, and the Holy Ghost: and these three are one."

The Hebrew word Elohiym (GOD, in plural) refers to the Father, the Son, and the Holy Spirit, but the verb is in the singular in every case where the plural form of God, "Elohiym," appears. Examples of what God says about Himself: "I, the LORD God," (I, YHWH Elohiym—not "we," YHWH and Elohiym), or "*I am* the LORD your God," (I am YHVH your Elohiym—not "we are" YHWH and Elohiym).

Since the Bible declares itself to be God's Word, it doesn't "argue" about God. The Bible clearly says that His ways and thoughts are far above our thoughts, but that through the Holy Spirit we can learn to understand what He has done for us and how great His love is toward us and thus believe in Him. God has given us a simple way, one way, a narrow way. Let no one confuse you about that. Jesus said, "I am the way, the truth and the life" (John 14:6). He said in John 17:3, "...this is eternal life, to know thee the only true God and Jesus Christ whom thou hast sent."

Just because you may previously have believed the false teachings of the LDS Church doesn't mean that you cannot now accept the truth from God's Word, the Bible.

Chapter 12

OUR TESTIMONY

Dennis Higley

I, Dennis, grew up in an LDS family, a sixth-generation Mormon. My parents were always active temple-going Mormons, and the same was expected of me. I never had a problem believing in the Mormon story, and was very happy when I was called on a mission to Finland, where I served faithfully for two and a half years. After my mission, I married Rauni in the Salt Lake LDS Temple and started serving in the ward and stake. I was called to be an Elder's Quorum president while still in my early twenties, and held teaching and leadership positions from that time. I was only in my thirties when I was ordained a High Priest and called to serve on the Stake High Council. Being busy in the Church and its activities and doing a lot of temple work in addition to my ward and stake positions took all my free time. It was Rauni who started to point out that there were problems with Mormon claims, and that we should check them out.

Rauni Higley

I, Rauni, was a convert to the LDS Church in Finland, where I served a "full-time mission" before coming to the States. I began working as a translator for the Finnish language in the Church Offices almost immediately after arrival in Salt Lake City, and I worked as a translator and language coordinator for the LDS Church over 14 years. Translation work gave me an opportunity to study Mormon history from many books not generally available to the membership of the Church. I began to question when I saw so many changes in the Church doctrines and contradictions between its scriptures and writings of the prophets and the high leadership of the Church. It became obvious to me that the Church was hiding a lot of important information from its membership.

I had teaching positions both in the Sunday School and in the Relief Society and also served many years on the Stake Relief Society Board. However, when the problems in Church doctrine became too much for me to accept, I suggested to Dennis that we should compare Mormon doctrine to the doctrine of the Bible to see if they matched. This was a serious question; if Mormonism was not the truth, then our eternal life and salvation were in danger.

In these pages, we have briefly presented some of the problems we found, which caused us eventually to separate from the LDS Church. Through a long study, we came to accept the Bible as the "infallible Word of God," and the Jesus of the Bible as our Lord and Savior.

The Road to Emmaus

As Mormons, we accepted the statement in the Articles of Faith that says we "believe the Bible as far as it is translated correctly." It started to bother us, because it seemed unreasonable to say that, yet not clarify where the translation might be incorrect. If the Church knew that it was incorrect, why didn't the Church correct it? The LDS Church as an organization employs a large number of translators covering a majority of the world's languages. The Hebrew text for the Old Testament as well as the Greek text for the New Testament are available, and even the Septuagint, the Greek translation of the Old Testament. (It was translated from the Hebrew about 270 BC. Greek was "the language of the world" at the time. This Greek version of the Old Testament was in common use at the time of Christ.) Most of the quotations from the Old Testament in the Greek New Testament are from the Septuagint. It is quite obvious that the Septuagint, and thus the Hebrew Old Testament as well, are correct, since Jesus Christ quoted from them and by doing so authenticated them.

On the road to Emmaus, Jesus said to His disciples, "O fools, and slow of heart to believe all that the prophets have spoken.... And beginning at Moses and all the prophets, he expounded unto them in all the scriptures the things concerning himself" (Luke 24:25-27).

Notice that He started from Moses, i.e., Genesis, and went through all the prophets (in other words, the entire Old

Testament), explaining that it all was written about Him. He did not mention any mistranslation in the Septuagint, or any missing books or mistaken scriptures. The Old Testament was complete in 400 BC and, as we have already mentioned, a complete canon in Greek (the Septuagint) about 270 years before Christ was born.

Jesus himself assured us (Matthew 5:18) that "...till heaven and earth pass, not one jot or one tittle shall pass" from His Word until all is fulfilled. (A "jot" and a "tittle" are the smallest parts of the letters, like dotting an "i" or crossing a "t.") Heaven and earth have not passed away, so we have His promise that we can trust His Word to be correct and complete.

Some Surprising Conclusions

When we came to the conclusion that we could trust the Bible and accept it as the infallible Word of God, it made a huge difference. We learned from it that what Mormon doctrine says about God is not the Bible doctrine of God. Mormon doctrine teaches that God was once a man who had a father—who had a father, and so on. According to the Bible, God is not a man (Numbers 23:19); there were no other gods before Him nor will there be after Him (Isaiah 43:10); the God of the Bible says that He doesn't even know any other gods. (Isaiah 44:8). That should make it clear to everyone that God was not first a man who had a father before him and also that men will not become gods.

Jesus, whom we had accepted as Mormons, is not the Jesus of the Bible. Jesus of the Bible is literally God Almighty, who became a man to redeem us (Isaiah 7:14; 9:6). We learned that He created everything, including Lucifer (Colossians 1:16), He is not a brother of human spirits nor a brother of Lucifer. He is the only Way, the Truth and the Life (John 14:6; Acts 4:12). His salvation is a gift, so no one can boast of earning it (Ephesians 2:8, 9); but one must know Him, as John 17:3 says. If we do not know that He is God, we will die in our sins, as He himself said in John 8:24. Doing good deeds in Jesus' name without having a relationship with the true Jesus Christ, will not benefit anyone (Matthew 7:22-23).

We could also see that there is no second chance (for the dead), since Jesus said in Luke 16:26, when speaking about the rich man and Lazarus, both of whom had died, "that there is a great gulf fixed; so that they which would pass from hence to you cannot; neither can they pass to us...." That means no missionary work on the other side. They cannot pass across that gulf. Hebrews 9:27 says, "It is appointed unto men once to die, but after this the judgment." After death comes judgment, not a second chance.

Psalm 49:7 says also, "None of them can by any means redeem his brother, or give to God a ransom for Him." Nothing we can do, after someone is dead, will help him. But the Bible says that we should "...exhort one another daily, while it is called Today....Today, if you will hear his voice, harden not your hearts..." Hebrews 3:13-15).

Our plea to you

God's way is very simple. If you would like to receive the truth, may we suggest that you go to God in prayer and tell Him that you want to denounce all false ways and false views of Him, which you may even have promoted, and that you now accept Him and His ways, and ask His guidance in understanding His Word, the Bible.

Ask God to search your heart and help you to understand that you cannot earn your salvation, but that you will accept it as a gift from God, as Ephesians 2:8, 9 says. Recognize that you are a sinner worthy only of the judgment of God and that you now want to receive the true Jesus Christ of the Bible into your heart and life, for you now believe that Jesus has paid the penalty for all your sins, past, present and future—when, hanging on the cross, He declared "It is finished" (in Greek, literally "Paid in full")—and that you now want to solely serve only Him. Ask God to help you to grow in the grace and knowledge of the true Savior, Jesus Christ (2 Peter 3:18). Amen.

Please visit us online at:
www.hismin.com

Notes

Notes